A Doll's House

A Drama in Three Acts

Samuel Adamson

A SAMUEL FRENCH ACTING EDITION

SAMUEL FRENCH

FOUNDED 1830

SAMUELFRENCH-LONDON.CO.UK
SAMUELFRENCH.COM

ISBN 978-0-573-01951-7

www.samuelfrench-london.co.uk

www.samuelfrench.com

FOR AMATEUR PRODUCTION ENQUIRIES

UNITED KINGDOM AND WORLD
EXCLUDING NORTH AMERICA
plays@SamuelFrench-London.co.uk
020 7255 4302/01

Each title is subject to availability from Samuel French,

depending upon country of performance.

A DOLL'S HOUSE

This version was first performed at the Southwark Playhouse, London, on 6th November 2003 with the following cast:

Nora	Kananu Kirimi
Anne-Marie	Jan Carey
Torvald	Ian Dunn
Kristine	Jennifer Hennessey
Dr Rank	Tim Preece
Krogstad	Paul Wyett
Ivor	William Camfield/Irfan Khan
Emmy	Meron Tilahun/Shauni Rixon

Directed by Thea Sharrock
Direction assisted by Claire Lovett
Designed by Rachel Blues
Lighting designed by Johanna Town
Sound designed by Carolyn Downing

CHARACTERS

Nora Helmer
Torvald Helmer
Kristine Linde
Nils Krogstad
Dr Rank
Anne-Marie, the housekeeper and nanny
Ivor, Torvald's and Nora's son
Emmy, their daughter

The action takes place in the living-room of Torvald's and Nora's flat

ACT I Christmas Eve. Morning
ACT II Christmas Day. Early Evening
ACT III Boxing Day. Evening

Time — late nineteenth century

ADAPTOR'S NOTE

This English-language *A Doll's House* was commissioned by Thea Sharrock, artistic director of the tiny, cash-strapped Southwark Playhouse in London, who wanted an actable, pared-down, colloquial text for her production to celebrate the 10th anniversary of the theatre in 2003. I take full responsibility for the minor cuts and embellishments demanded by this *ad hoc* enterprise, all of which are retained in the published text for the benefit of amateur companies. None of these changes are attributable to Charlotte Barslund, who provided the exemplary literal translation from which I made my version. I'm grateful to Claire Lovett, Rachel Blues, Kananu Kirimi and Thea for their suggestions and contributions.

Samuel Adamson
London, February 2005

ACT I

Christmas Eve. Morning

A comfortable room, tasteful but modest, with a piano and a stove. There are several doors: one leads to Torvald's study; one to a room for Nora and then to the children's rooms; another to the hall and front door. The letter-box is visible when the door to the living-room is open. It has a glass front but can't be opened without a key

Nora enters from the hall, laden with parcels

Nora Ding-a-ling? (*She hums*)

Anne-Marie enters

Is it safe?
Anne-Marie Yes, Mrs Nora, they're playing in their rooms.
Nora The boy at the door, Anne-Marie — here's half a ... Oh, he deserves a tip, give him a crown. And say thank you.

Anne-Marie exits to the hall

Nora takes her overcoat off and bustles about, laughing to herself

Anne-Marie enters the room with a basket and a Christmas tree

Hide it somewhere safe, the children mustn't see it till it's been trimmed.

Anne-Marie nods and exits with the tree

Nora takes a bag of macaroons from her pocket and eats two. She gingerly approaches the door to Torvald's study. She hums

Torvald (*off*) Who's twittering? Not the lark?
Nora The lark, yes. (*She busies herself with the parcels*)
Torvald (*off*) That couldn't be the squirrel, darting about out there?
Nora The squirrel, it is.
Torvald (*off*) You mean squirrel's home already?

Nora Yes, why don't you ... (*She puts the macaroons back in her pocket and wipes her mouth*) Why don't you come and see what I've bought?

Torvald (*off*) Do not disturb.

A moment

Torvald enters with pen in hand

I beg your pardon? "Bought"? All this? She's been on another spending spree, then?

Nora Well. Yes. She has Torvald. But this Christmas we don't have to worry, do we? We can splash a little?

Torvald Not to excess.

Nora A bit of excess. With your new big salary. We're going to be rich.

Torvald Not till New Year, and I don't get paid till the end of March.

Nora So what? We can borrow till then.

Torvald. Nora. (*He pinches her ear*) Let's see: I borrow a thousand crowns today, you splash about this Christmas, and on New Year's Eve I'm struck dead by a roof tile.

Nora (*her hand to his mouth*) Stop, Torvald, stop.

Torvald It could happen.

Nora Well I wouldn't worry about my debts, then.

Torvald And my creditors?

Nora I couldn't care a whit about them. Strangers. Complete strangers.

Torvald Little Nora. That's enough. How many times do I have to say it? Never borrow. Build a home on debts — then watch it rot. Be patient. We've held on for this long. Three more months, that's all.

Nora Yes, Torvald. You're right.

Torvald And now the lark has lost her song. Squirrel's droopy-eyed.

Nora isn't looking at him. Torvald takes his wallet out

Hmn, I wonder what it is that I have *here*?

Nora Money!

Torvald Yes, yes, I know how expensive it is to run a house at Christmas. (*He hands her some banknotes*)

Nora (*counting*) Ten, thank you, Torvald; twenty, thank you; thirty, I'll stretch it, Torvald; forty, I'll watch every last ——

Torvald Do that.

Nora Promise — but look. Bargains. Trousers for Ivor, and a sword, and a trumpet; a doll for Emmy, she'll rip its head off, but never mind, and a cradle; dress-material for Anne-Marie, and some scarves, I really should have found something special for her, dear old thing ——

Torvald And what's in *this* one?

Nora No, Torvald. Tonight, tonight, tonight!

Torvald But it seems to me the lark hasn't bought anything to line her own nest?

Nora Me? Pfff. I don't need a thing.

Torvald Really? There must be something. Something that isn't extravagant.

Nora Not that I can think of. Except.

Torvald Hmn?

Nora Well if you think I should have something, if you'd like to give me something, then ——

Torvald Twitter, twitter.

Nora — then you could give me money, Torvald. Only what you can spare. Then when I get around to it, I'll buy something for myself ——

Torvald Nora.

Nora — because it'd look lovely on the Christmas tree tonight, wrapped in gold paper, wouldn't it?

Torvald Yes, and what will the lark go on, the day after tomorrow?

Nora I know, I know, a "spree", but do it my way, Torvald, because don't you see: then, I'll have time to think about what I really want. Isn't that clever?

Torvald Genius.

Nora Please.

Torvald It'll slip through your fingers. You'll fritter it away on some useless thing for the house ——

Nora But ——

Torvald — and then I'll have to find more. And after that, more. Isn't that the truth? (*He puts his arms around her waist*) Spree after spree. A man could lose a fortune, keeping his little lark ...

Nora. You're being cruel. I look after the pennies.

Torvald. We just never see the crowns.

Nora (*hums*) Torvald, Torvald. You just don't know how much it all costs. Spare a thought for we squirrels.

Torvald Little Nora. Like father, like daughter. All the time scheming and scrounging, and nothing to show for it. You get your hands on money, it disappears. Well, when something's hereditary ... Yes, it runs through your veins.

Nora Oh, I wish I had more of Pa's character.

Torvald You're perfect just as you are. Hmn. My sly, sly lark.

Nora Me?

Torvald. Look me in the eyes, Nora Helmer.

She does. Torvald wags his finger

No cake in town today?

Nora I don't know what you mean.

Torvald No quick visit to the *pâtisserie*?

Nora No, Torvald, honestly I ——

Torvald Just for a little cream puff?

Nora Never.

Torvald Only to chew on a macaroon or two?

Nora But I made a promise, Torvald. I ——

Torvald Don't panic, Nora. You keep your festive secrets secret. Tonight the Christmas tree will throw light over everything.

Nora You didn't forget to invite Dr Rank?

Torvald I did. It doesn't matter, I'll ask him this morning. I've ordered fine wine. Yes, I think it's going to be an evening to remember, Nora. I can't wait.

Nora. I can't either, Torvald — the children are so excited!

Torvald What a thing. Security. A safe job, a good salary.

Nora The best thing in the world.

Torvald Better than last Christmas, hmn? You locked away at night working your fingers off: flowers for the tree, home-made surprises. Made the best of it, didn't you, for three whole weeks — I've never been so bored in my life.

Nora I wasn't bored.

Torvald laughs

Stop. Stop it, Torvald, it wasn't my fault the stupid cat found it all and ripped it to shreds; anyway none of that matters.

Torvald. No. It's all history. This year I've got you to myself.

Nora History. That was then and this is now. It's almost miraculous. (*She takes him by the arm*) Now, there are piles of things to talk about: so much to organize and see to and change. Once Christmas is done with, I want to ——

The doorbell rings

Oh. Who's that? Pfff.

Torvald I'm not at home.

Anne-Marie enters from the hall

Anne-Marie A lady to see you, Mrs Helmer. She didn't give her name.

Nora Show her in.

Anne-Marie And the doctor's arrived, sir, I sent him to your study.

Torvald nods and exits to his study

Anne-Marie shows Kristine Linde into the room. She's dressed in travelling clothes

Anne-Marie exits

Kristine Hallo. You don't recognize me?
Nora Of course I recognize you. (*She doesn't but then, realizing*) Kristine?

Kristine nods. Nora squeals

Kristine Hallo, Nora.
Nora Kristine! Come in, come in, come in!
Kristine Thank you.
Nora You can hardly blame me for — Kristine, you look so — I mean ——
Kristine It's been nine years. Ten.
Nora Nine. Yes, it has, hasn't it? I can't believe you're here.
Kristine Nor can I, really.
Nora But all this way in the middle of winter?
Kristine I arrived on the steamer this morning.
Nora In time for Christmas! With us. Well, that just completes the picture. How exciting.

She gestures for Kristine to take off her coat, then helps her with it

Kristine Thank you.
Nora Sit. No, no, there. (*She clutches Kristine's hands*) Oh, Kristine. It is you. A bit pale, that's all. Thin.
Kristine Old, Nora.
Nora Yes, old — old*er* — but it doesn't show that much —— (*She claps her hand to her mouth*) My mouth. I'm sorry. Kristine. I'm so sorry.
Kristine What do you mean?
Norah Your husband.
Kristine Oh. That was three years ago.
Nora I read about his funeral and I wanted to write — believe me — but I put it off and put it off, there was always something happening, something to ——
Kristine Don't be silly. I understand.
Nora No, I'm a monster. No excuse. Oh, Kristine. Did he leave you much money?
Kristine No.
Nora Children?
Kristine No.
Nora Nothing?

Kristine Not even heartache.

Nora But I don't understand. How can that be true?

Kristine It's not so unusual, Nora.

Nora Nothing? All alone, by yourself? That must have been terrible for you. Oh, Kris, Kris. Things couldn't have been better for me. You must meet Ivor and Emmy, my children, but later, talk to me now, tell me everything.

Kristine No, you first.

Nora I won't go first, I'm not going to think of myself today, only of you, only Kristine. Just one thing. Our amazing turn-of-events, you may have even heard about it ——

Kristine shakes her head

My husband is the new manager of the bank.

Kristine Manager? Oh! How lucky.

Nora I know. Well, life as a lawyer is hard, let me tell you, especially if you're picking and choosing your cases, only taking the ones that are above-board, which is Torvald to a T — and I completely agree with him. But that's over. He starts at the bank in the New Year. Enormous salary. Bonuses, dividends. Kris, everything is different now. We'll be rich, we won't have to worry any more. I feel as light as a feather. A new life.

Kristine (*smiling*) Yes, how nice to be able to afford everything you need.

Nora Not just what we need. Pots and pots of money.

Kristine You haven't changed at all, Nora. You goose. I remember at school you were exactly the same; you loved money, you used to spend it like there was no tomorrow.

Nora You could be Torvald! (*She wags her finger*) Well, Nora isn't the goose you think she is, Kris. We've struggled. And I had to do my bit. Yes, me. Sewing, that kind of thing. And more. Torvald quit the civil service after we got married — he had to, he wasn't earning enough there — but after he began working for himself, things got on top of him. Long, long hours. He got ill. Too ill, Kris. The next thing you know, he's staring at death. We had to go somewhere warm. Italy.

Kristine With the children?

Nora Yes, can you imagine? But needs must. It was bit of a thrill, really. And it saved Torvald's life. So I think that was worth every crown, don't you? It was worth every last one of those four thousand eight hundred crowns.

Kristine That much? Thank God you had it.

Nora Thank God Pa had it.

Kristine Oh.

Nora Yes, and *he* was on death's door himself then. Both of them, deadly sick at the same time. Think of it, Kristine: I couldn't go home to look after my own father. My Torvald needed me so much. I never saw Pa again. Poor soul.

Kristine You loved him. I know.

Nora I can't bear to think about it. It's the worst thing that's ever happened to me.

Kristine And so after that, Italy?

Nora Yes. Doctor's orders. We had the money; so we left.

Kristine But, Nora, Torvald's all right now, isn't he?

Nora Completely cured!

Kristine So the doctor, the man who was in the hall ———?

Nora Doctor Rank? He's not here to treat anyone, he's our friend, he's spends his life with us. Torvald's fit as a fiddle. And so are the children and so am I. (*She claps*) Good Lord, good Lord, Kris, isn't it almost miraculous to be alive? I'm ecstatic. (*She puts her arms on Kristine's knee*) I'm a monster. Me, me, me. Please don't be angry. Why did you marry your husband, if you didn't love him?

Kristine My mother was very ill; my brothers weren't old enough to leave home then, and they needed looking after. I didn't think I had a choice.

Nora Yes. I see. So he was rich?

Kristine Quite, I thought. But his business wasn't secure. When he died it went under. I did what I could. I looked after a school for a while, then I ran a shop. In fact I've been working every day for three years. But that's all over. Mother died, and the boys have their own lives now.

Nora Relief.

Kristine No. You see, no-one needs me. I can't stand that town any more; it's so cut off. I have to find a way to engage with — something. I thought maybe I could find a job here. In an office. Anything.

Nora Oh no, Kris, drudgery, pure drudgery, and you already look half dead. No, what you should have done is headed south to a spa.

Kristine It's a pity I don't have a pa to pay for that, isn't it?

Nora I'm sorry.

Kristine No, no, I am. It's me. I've become so selfish. I feel completely useless, but life goes on, doesn't it, you have to get by? Seems I'd grasp at anything. When you told me about your bit of luck — can you believe this? — I didn't think of you, I thought of myself.

Nora Oh? Oh, you wonder if Torvald might be able to help you?

Kristine nods

Not another word, Kristine. You leave it to me. I'll make everything just right for him, then I'll suggest it very subtly. Yes, I'd love to help you.

Kristine Thank you, Nora. You've always been so snug and comfortable; I didn't think you'd understand.

Nora What did you say ———?

Kristine Of course, there is your sewing. Back-breaking, I know.

Nora You should mind your mouth. You're like the rest of them. You all think I know nothing about serious things.

Kristine Nora ——

Nora Nothing about how hard life can be.

Kristine You just told me all about ——

Nora All about what? Pfff. I didn't tell you the special thing.

Kristine What, exactly?

Nora You don't take me seriously, Kristine.

Kristine That's not true.

Nora You're so pleased with yourself for looking after your mother and brothers ——

Kristine I'm proud of that; shouldn't I be?

Nora Yes, you should: and so why shouldn't I be proud of the special thing I've done?

Kristine Oh?

Nora Sssh, Torvald mustn't hear. Never, ever. No-one can know except you, Kris. (*She pulls her close*) I saved Torvald's life.

Kristine You ——

Nora Italy — sshh — Italy. Torvald would have died if we hadn't gone.

Kristine Yes and your father gave you the money ——

Nora Pa? That's what Torvald thinks. It's what they all think. Pa didn't give us a penny. I got the money. Four thousand eight hundred crowns. What do you say to that?

Kristine Did you win a lottery?

Nora Don't be stupid, would that require talent?

Kristine Well where ——?

Nora Tra-la-la.

Kristine You couldn't have borrowed it.

Nora Oh?

Kristine A wife needs her husband's permission to borrow.

Nora But if the wife has a head for business.

Kristine Nora, what are you saying?

Nora Forget it, who said I borrowed it? I could have got it any number of ways. When a girl's as gorgeous as I am ...

Kristine You goose.

Nora Kris smells a secret ...

Kristine Nora, have you done something mad?

Nora What's mad about wanting to save your husband's life?

Kristine If you never told him ——

Nora Good God. You don't understand. He couldn't know! He wasn't allowed to know anything. The doctors told *me* he was at death's door; that it was Italy, or Ivor and Emmy would be fatherless. Obviously I tried to coax him first, sweet-talk him into it. "I need a holiday", "Nora and the children need to see some sun". Then I suggested a loan; that sent him wild, Kris. He had his "Duty not to give in" to me; he called me "giddy", *giddy* he said! Well, I thought: "You, sir, cannot die". So I found my own way.

Kristine Didn't your father tell Torvald the money wasn't from him?

Nora Pa never knew. I thought of telling him, but he was so ill, and before long, it didn't matter. Pa had died.

Kristine And you never told Torvald?

Nora For God's sake, no. Torvald's a man, he's so strict about money, can you imagine how mortified he'd be if he knew he owed me something? That'd be the end of us. It would twist everything out of shape. I'd have to kiss it all goodbye.

Kristine Will you ever tell him?

Nora Maybe. One day. Ages from now when my looks have worn off a bit ——

Kristine laughs

Don't. I mean when Torvald doesn't want me so much; when he doesn't care about me dressing-up, playing and dancing for him. Then it could be handy to have an ace up my ... No, no, won't happen. So, Kristine, my special secret? Seems I have my uses? It's been terrible, my God; "repayments", "quarterly interest", all these business things, it's another world. And payment days come around so quickly. I've had to scrimp and save. I couldn't use any of the housekeeping money, Torvald has his standards, and my children have to have good clothes.

Kristine So you've gone without?

Nora (*nods*) Whenever Torvald gave me money, I put half aside. And Nora wore the plainest clothes. Luckily I look good in anything. Torvald's never noticed. Still, Kris. Lovely things are lovely, aren't they?

Kristine They are.

Nora There's more. Last Christmas I had a stroke of luck and got some copying work. I locked myself in my room and burnt the midnight oil; I wrote and wrote; I felt so drained; but what a thrill, to work and earn — like a man.

Kristine How much have you paid off?

Nora Hard to say. It's complicated. Every penny I've saved has gone towards the debt. Grrr, sometimes it's sent me round the ...! I used to dream an old man with pots of money had fallen madly in love with me ——

Kristine What?

Nora Pfff, don't be silly — and that he'd kicked up his heels, and at the reading of the will they announced, "All the old man's pots of money go this instant to the gorgeous Mrs Nora Helmer".

Kristine Nora, who is he?

Nora Good God, Kris, he isn't real, just a game I played when I'd run out of ways to get cash. And I don't care a whit now, the old tease, let him keep the will … (*She jumps*) Oh, Kris, what a thing not to have a worry in the world! To roll around on the nursery floor with Ivor and Emmy, to live in this house, with that chair just over there where Torvald likes it! And spring's round the corner, blue open skies, and trips — the sea, the sea. Yes. Almost miraculous.

The doorbell rings

Kristine I must go.
Nora I wouldn't hear of it. It's probably for Torvald.

Anne-Marie enters

Anne-Marie A gentleman to see your husband, Mrs Helmer, but ——
Nora (*to Kristine*) Bank business, probably. (*To Anne-Marie*) What's his name?

Krogstad appears in the doorway

Krogstad It's me, Mrs Helmer.

Kristine starts at Krogstad's appearance, and turns away

Nora (*whispers*) What are you doing here?
Krogstad As you said: bank business.
Nora You?
Krogstad I've just heard your husband's our new manager.
Nora Yes?
Krogstad Which makes him my employer. Nothing important.
Nora Oh. He's with someone. But you could try. Down the hall.

Krogstad exits

Nora closes the hall door behind him. She busies herself at the stove

Kristine Nora, who was that?
Nora A Mr Krogstad.
Kristine Krogstad.
Nora You know him?
Kristine Of course. We both do. He was a clerk at our town solicitor's, wasn't he?

Nora Yes, probably.

Kristine I haven't seen him in years. He looks so different.

Nora Ghastly marriage. So I've heard. The wife's dead. A number of children. There, now it's burning.

Kristine And now he does some kind of work — business, on the side? Is that true?

Nora I wouldn't know.

Dr Rank backs out of Torvald's study

Dr Rank — no, not another word, your wife can look after me — (*he turns and notices Kristine*) if it weren't for the fact I'm interrupting her, as well.

Nora Don't be silly. Dr Rank, Mrs Kristine Linde.

Dr Rank A familiar name in this house. Oh, it's you! I passed you on the street, didn't I?

Kristine Yes, I'd stopped to catch my breath.

Dr Rank Are you a bit out of sorts?

Kristine Tired, that's all.

Dr Rank And a tour of the living-rooms of our town is the prescribed restorative, not bed?

Kristine I'm looking for work.

Dr Rank How perverse.

Kristine We have to live, Doctor.

Dr Rank So I've heard.

Nora Stop it, you. You want to live as much as anyone.

Dr Rank Correct. "I'm miserable as sin, but keep me alive". That's what my patients say. All the ill say it. And people who are perfectly healthy but irrevocably bad say it, too: people like that stinking so-and-so in there with Helmer.

Kristine starts in spite of herself

Nora What do you mean?

Dr Rank Krogstad, a lawyer: you wouldn't know him. Trouble-maker. Still, apparently even those who can't make the distinction between right and wrong have their right to live.

Nora What does he want to see Torvald about?

Dr Rank The bank.

Nora I didn't even know Krog — Mr Krogstad — had anything to do with the bank.

Dr Rank Yes, he's a junior clerk. There's a phenomenon here, Mrs Linde: bad men in good jobs. They stay nice and warm, the healthy are shut out to freeze. Is it the same where you're from?

Kristine But we have to bring the sick indoors.
Dr Rank Of course I keep forgetting society is one big hospital.

Nora, lost in her own thoughts, laughs and claps her hands

You there? Do you even know what society is?
Nora Me, I don't care a fig for it. No, something else, something very funny.
Everyone at the bank will answer to Torvald now, won't they, Dr Rank?
Dr Rank That made you laugh out loud?
Nora Forget it. Forget it! (*She hums*) Imagine: we —Torvald — has all that
authority over all those people. Care for a macaroon, Doctor?
Dr Rank Aren't they illegal in these parts?
Nora Kristine gave them to me.

Kristine begins to protest

Sshh-ssshh, you couldn't know about Torvald's Law Against Macaroons,
could you? It's a thing he has about my teeth. One can't kill us. What do
you think, Dr Rank? Don't answer, open wide. (*She pops one in his mouth*)
Kris. And a tiny one for me. (*She eats one. She eats another*) Mmn. Do you
know, there's only one thing left now that I'm dying to do.
Dr Rank Oh yes?
Nora Actually, it's something I'm dying to say. When Torvald's in the room.
Dr Rank What's stopping you?
Nora It's rude.
Dr Rank Better keep your lips sealed, then. Or at least try it out on us first.
Nora I'm dying to say: bloody hell.
Dr Rank Heavens.
Kristine Nora!

A noise from Torvald's study alerts Dr Rank

Dr Rank Here he comes. Go ahead.
Nora (*hiding the macaroons*) Sssshhh!

Torvald enters from his study, overcoat and hat in hand

Did you see him off, Torvald?
Torvald Yes.
Nora Good, introductions. I'd like you to meet Kris. She's just arrived in
town.
Torvald Kris ——?
Nora Mrs Linde, Torvald, Mrs Kristine Linde, an old friend of mine.

Torvald Really?

Kristine Since we were girls.

Nora And you'll never believe it, Torvald, she's come all this way to speak to you ——

Torvald Me?

Kristine I ——

Nora Kristine is a virtuoso in offices. And what she wants more than anything is to work for a gifted man so she can learn even more.

Torvald Really? Clever thinking.

Nora And then she heard you'd become manager of the bank — through a friend of a friend and a telegram — so she caught the first steamer out and here she is. So, Torvald. Could you find her a job? For me?

Torvald It's possible. You're a widow?

Kristine Yes.

Torvald Experienced?

Kristine Very.

Torvald As luck would have it ——

Nora Perfect. You see?

Torvald — as luck would have it, Mrs Linde, something should crop up soon.

Kristine Oh, thank you, very much ——

Torvald No need for that — (*he puts on his overcoat*) — though you'll have to excuse me now.

Dr Rank I'll come with you.

Dr Rank gets his coat from the hall and warms it on the stove. Kristine puts on hers

Nora Don't be long, Torvald.

Torvald An hour at most.

Nora You're not going, Kris?

Kristine I have to find somewhere to live.

Torvald We'll walk together, then.

Nora We're shoulder-to-shoulder here, otherwise you know ——

Kristine Don't be ridiculous, Nora. Goodbye. And thank you.

They move into the hall noisily. The conversations overlap

Nora Goodbye, goodbye! Come back this evening everybody ...!

Ivor and Emmy run in to the living-room with their paintings. Anne-Marie follows

Emmy Mummy?

Nora You too, Dr Rank.
Dr Rank I mightn't be up to that.
Nora Wrap up warm, you will be.
Ivor Where are you going!

During the following, Torvald and Dr Rank try to make their escape. Ivor and Emmy rush towards the hall

Nora Oh, look who's come to see us at last, my boy, my girl! (*She kisses them*)
Ivor I painted this for you — see, Mummy?
Anne-Marie Ivor ... Emmy ...
Nora Here's Ivor, Kris, isn't he handsome?
Kristine How do you do?
Nora And this is little Emmy. Say hallo to Mrs Linde.
Dr Rank We'll catch our deaths out here.
Torvald March on, Mrs Linde. Mothers only.

Torvald, Rank and Kristine manage to extricate themselves from the commotion and exit

Nora, Ivor, Emmy and Anne-Marie move back into the living-room. Nora closes the door to the hall

Nora Look at you two, haven't you been good this morning? Paint on your cheeks, like funny clowns!
Ivor Look, a snow-fight.
Nora Oh, how clever.
Emmy Mummy, Mummy, I saw a dog from the window, it got into a fight.
Nora Huh! Did it? I hope it wasn't Mr Stenborg's ...
Ivor Here's a man on a sledge.
Nora I can almost imagine being there.
Anne-Marie Come along, children.
Nora Please no, Anne-Marie, I'll spend some time with them.
Anne-Marie Are you sure?
Nora Please let me. It's so much fun. You rest for a while.

Anne-Marie exits

Nora looks at the paintings and lets them fall to the floor as she tries to wipe paint off Emmy's cheeks. Ivor is attracted to the presents

Emmy Let's dance, Mummy.

Nora In a minute, let me wipe this mess off your cheeks ...!
Ivor What are these?
Nora No, Ivor.
Ivor What's in this one?
Nora I'm not going to tell you, because it's something frightening and
horrible!
Ivor It is not!
Nora Yes it is, but you won't see what till tonight!
Emmy Is mine frightening and horrible?
Nora Yours is even worse!
Ivor Mummy!
Nora Patience, patience, patience! Hide-and-seek! I'm coming to find you!
Ten, nine —

*Ivor and Emmy rush off, forgetting about the presents and paintings. Nora
puts her hands over her eyes and counts. Lots of excitement as the children
find places to hide*

Ten, nine, I'm coming to get you, eight ...

There's a knock on the door to the hall during this but no-one hears it

Seven, I'm coming to get you, six, five, I'm coming to get you ...

Krogstad opens the door and enters

Four, three ... Watch out, I'm coming to find you ... Two ——
Krogstad Mrs Helmer.

Nora screams

I beg your pardon.
Nora You frightened the life out of me.
Ivor Mummy?
Krogstad I'm sorry. Somebody left the front door open.
Nora My husband isn't at home, Mr Krogstad.
Krogstad Yes.
Nora Well then.
Krogstad It's not your husband I want to talk to.

Nora stares at him

Emmy Mummy?

Nora Anne-Marie!
Ivor Is he going to hurt you?
Nora No. Go to your room.

Anne-Marie enters and takes the Children away

Off you go. We'll play in a minute, I promise. Quickly ...

She sees Anne-Marie and the Children out

They exit

Silence

It's not the first of the month.
Krogstad No, it's the twenty-fourth. How happy your Christmas is depends on you.
Nora What do you want today? It's Christmas Eve, you can't expect me to——
Krogstad This is a different issue.

Nora stares, confounded

I was sitting in the café on the corner a moment ago. And your husband walked straight past the window ——
Nora So?
Krogstad With a woman.
Nora And?
Krogstad Was it Kristine Linde?
Nora Yes.
Krogstad She's here?
Nora Yes.
Krogstad Your old friend?
Nora That's nothing to do with you.
Krogstad I knew Mrs Linde once.
Nora I know.
Krogstad Ah. I see. Well, I won't waste any more time. Is Mrs Linde to have a job at the bank?
Nora Who do you think you are, asking me questions like that, Mr Krogstad? You work under my husband. If you want to know, then yes, she's about to start a job there. And I helped her get it.
Krogstad Ah. Clever me.
Nora I do have some sway over things, you know. Being a woman doesn't mean ... Anyway, if you ask me, bank juniors — inferiors — should take care. They should be careful not to upset someone who is ... Someone who has, um ——

Krogstad "Sway"?
Nora Exactly.

Silence

Krogstad Mrs Helmer. I'd like to ask you a favour. Would you use some of
your influence to help me?
Nora What are you talking about?
Krogstad Please. I want to keep my job at the bank.
Nora Why shouldn't you?
Krogstad Please don't pretend to be whiter than white. A job for Mrs Linde;
and I'm being bullied out. Now, who could be responsible for all that?
Nora Oh no, I promise, that's not ——
Krogstad I haven't got time for this: stop it while you still can.
Nora Mr Krogstad. There's nothing I can do.
Krogstad You just said you had ——
Nora What on earth makes you think I could influence my husband like that?
Krogstad I've known Torvald for years. I'm sure he's as vulnerable to a little
henpecking as any other married man.
Nora How dare you? You know your way out.
Krogstad Very brave.
Nora You don't scare me any more. This'll all be over in the New Year.
Krogstad Mrs Helmer. I won't lose that job. I'll fight.
Nora Clearly.
Krogstad I'll fight with every fibre of my being. And you know why. Look
here. Yes, you know all about me, of course you do. Everyone knows the
dirty truth about Krogstad.
Nora Perhaps somebody once ——
Krogstad One lapse of judgement. It never even went to court, but they may
as well have thrown me in gaol. My name was mud. I had to do something,
so I became a "businessman", of sorts — hence our relationship. I've held
my head up, I'm not as bad as most. And I'd started to turn my back on it,
Mrs Helmer. I owe that to my boys. They're growing up. I don't care about
the money, it's *respect* I need, and that job was my new beginning. Now
Torvald Helmer wants to kick me into the dirt again.
Nora For God's sake, Mr Krogstad, I can't help.
Krogstad You can, you just don't want to. Maybe I'll have to force you.
Nora You'd never tell Torvald I owe you money?
Krogstad What if I did?
Nora It would be disgusting. (*She fights back tears*) That secret's my special
thing, it's my life; after everything, for you to tell him? — it would be so
bare and dirty, awful for me, it would ——
Krogstad "Awful"?

Nora Oh, go ahead, do it. Show your true colours. Your job will definitely be history then.

Krogstad I don't follow. There might be a household spat? A domestic squabble? Is *that* all you're worried about?

Nora Tell him, tell him. Torvald'll pay off the debt and you'll be dead to us.

Krogstad Mrs Helmer, I'm beginning to wonder if you've lost your memory? Or perhaps this isn't an act and you really know nothing about business? Listen. When your husband became ill, you came to me.

Nora nods

Four thousand eight hundred crowns. I agreed, on a few conditions. I think you were so desperate to get away you barely took any notice. Detail, Mrs Helmer, detail. I promised to find you the money against an IOU.

Nora And I signed it.

Krogstad And one of the conditions was that your father act as guarantor. So there was a further clause that *he* was required to sign.

Nora Yes. Pa did that.

Krogstad Required to sign, and *date*.

Nora nods

I gave you the IOU, you sent it to your father as agreed, and five or six days later I had it back, with his signature. So you got your money.

Nora And I've repaid you like clockwork.

Krogstad Yes, it doesn't keep time very well, that clock, but never mind. Things were difficult for you then, Mrs Helmer, correct? Your father was close to death?

Nora Yes!

Krogstad And when did he die? The exact date?

Nora The twenty-ninth of September.

Krogstad Good, that confirms it. The problem with that — (*he produces a piece of paper*) is this.

Nora What?

Krogstad Your father signed the IOU three days after he died.

Nora is silent

His signature. Dated the second of October. Uncanny.

Nora is silent

Perhaps you can clear it up?

Nora is silent

I also found an old letter your father once wrote me when I was a clerk. And the funny thing is, the handwriting on the IOU, here — "the second of October" — looks very different from the handwriting on the letter. Well, perhaps he forgot to date the document and someone else did it before his death became public. Harmless enough. It's the signature I'm interested in. It is a *bone fide* signature, of course? It was your father who signed this IOU, wasn't it?

Nora is silent for a second

Nora No. I signed Pa's name.

Krogstad Mrs Helmer. That's a very grave admission.

Nora I don't see why, you'll get your money.

Krogstad Why in God's name didn't you send it to him?

Nora He would have wanted to know what it was for. And I didn't want to tell him that Torvald was dying; I just couldn't make it worse for Pa, I couldn't. Not in a million years.

Krogstad You should have cancelled your trip.

Nora Torvald was deadly sick, it was life or death.

Krogstad It was fraud. You were swindling me.

Nora Well I didn't care about any of that, did I? I thought you were a horrible piece of work. All those hurdles of yours, all that "detail", when you knew how ill Torvald was.

Krogstad You don't have the faintest idea what you're guilty of, do you? A little lesson. There's no difference between your lapse and mine. And my reputation went to pieces.

Nora You're trying to tell me you did something brave to save your wife's life?

Krogstad The law doesn't care about the reason.

Nora The law's daft, then.

Krogstad If this goes to court — (*he holds up the paper*) you'll be judged by it, daft or not.

Nora I don't believe it. A daughter has the right to protect her dying father from heartache. A wife has the right to pull her husband back from the brink. There's not much I know about the law, but it says that somewhere. You can't be much of a lawyer, Mr Krogstad. You must be a very shabby lawyer.

Krogstad "Shabby"? Whatever you say. You don't know me as a lawyer, though. To you I'm a businessman. Tell me how shabby I am in *business*?

Silence

Do what you like. But if I'm kicked into the gutter again, you come with me.

He exits via the hall

Nora (*whispering*) Trying to — trying to frighten. Does he think I'm a child? (*She occupies herself by clearing up Ivor's paintings*) It can't be. For love. Love.

Ivor appears at Nora's door

Ivor Mummy?
Nora Yes! Ivor, you're not allowed to tell anyone about the stranger. He's gone. No-one, not even Daddy. Cross your heart.
Ivor Hide-and-seek again?

Nora shakes her head

You promised.
Nora I've got too much to do. Paint me another picture, good boy. Off you go, please.

She gently forces him out

He exits

She occupies herself with embroidery. She stops

Anne-Marie, the tree, now! (*She whispers*) Never. Never.

Anne-Marie enters with the Christmas tree

Anne-Marie Where would you like it?
Nora Over there, thank you. Keep the children away, please.
Anne-Marie Yes, Mrs Nora.

Anne-Marie exits

Nora starts decorating the tree with red ribbons

Lovely ... Red ... *Insolent.* Our perfect tree. Candles. Flowers. Whatever you want, Torvald, a song, a dance, anything ... Anything ...

Torvald enters from the hall. He has a bundle of papers under his arm

Torvald Who are you talking to?
Nora Oh! Back already.
Torvald Did anyone visit?

Nora No.
Torvald Strange. I saw Krogstad leaving the building.
Nora Who? Oh, yes, him. He popped his head round the corner.
Torvald Nora? He asked you to put in a good word for him, didn't he?

Nora nods

And you were to say it was your idea? And pretend he hadn't been here?
He asked you to do that?
Nora Mmn, but ——
Torvald Nora, how could you? A man like Krogstad? A promise to him and
then a lie to me?
Nora A lie?
Torvald You said no-one had been here. (*He wags his finger*) Little Nora,
little lark. Your song must be sweet, and pure, and full of truth. (*He puts
his hands around her waist*) Yes?

She nods. He lets her go

We'll forget it.

*He makes himself comfortable and reads his papers. Nora continues
decorating the tree*

Nora Torvald.
Torvald Nora?
Nora I can't wait for the fancy-dress party at the Stenborgs' on Boxing Day.
Torvald And I can't wait for your surprise.

He works. She approaches him

Nora Are you very busy, Torvald?
Torvald Mmn.
Nora The bank? Already?
Torvald The outgoing man's given me full discretion. I want to get on top
of things. A new budget, staff changes. No rest for me this Christmas.
Nora So that's why poor Krogstad ——
Torvald Nora.

He works. She plays with his hair

Nora If you weren't quite this busy, there's one thing I'd have quite liked
to …
Torvald Yes?

Nora You see I want to stun the Stenborgs at the party on Boxing Day and everything I think of is silly and you're a man of impeccable taste, so couldn't you take charge and decide what I should go as?

Torvald A-ha. The lark finally admits she has a broken wing. Do I have to come and put it right?

Nora Of course, Torvald, I'd be nothing if it weren't for you.

Torvald I'll think about it.

Nora Thank you. (*She goes back to the Christmas tree*) Red. Gorgeous.

Silence

Torvald. The thing Mr Krogstad did? Was it so wrong?

Torvald He forged signatures. You do know how serious that is?

Nora Perhaps he did it because he had to.

Torvald He's an idiot, in a world full of them. I've got a heart, Nora. I could forgive an idiot one crime.

Nora Yes, Torvald?

Torvald A fool can confess his sin, take his punishment.

Nora Punishment?

Torvald But Krogstad didn't do that. He wheedled his way out of it. He's a cheat. Corrupt. End of story.

Nora Corrupt because ——

Torvald He's guilty, Nora, and guilt makes men lie. Think about that. Big lies, little ones, every day. To their wives, their children — God help us, their children — that's the worst of it.

Nora Why?

Torvald Lies are diseases. The home's infected. The children don't even realize they're breathing in poison.

Nora But ——

Torvald I was a lawyer: I saw it again and again. So many youngsters who'd lost their way. Evil mothers, evil sons.

Nora Evil just because of their mothers?

Torvald Bad mothers are most often the cause of it; bad fathers, as well. I don't understand Krogstad, not at all. How can he go home every evening, week after week, year after year, happy to infect his own children? It's beyond corrupt. (*He holds his hands out to her*) Nora, you mustn't ask me to help him. No, give me your hand, I need a promise. Good. Understood. I can't have him near me. He makes me sick to the stomach.

Nora I've got a million things to do.

Torvald Yes, I should finish this report before dinner. And I'll think of your party-costume. And perhaps later there might be a little something for you to wrap in gold paper and hang on the Christmas tree. (*He puts his hand on her head*) My sweet, sweet lark.

He exits to his study and closes the door

Silence

Nora No. Not true. Never.

Anne-Marie enters through Nora's door

Anne-Marie Mrs Nora, the children would love to see you.
Nora They mustn't come near me. Stay with them, Anne-Marie.

Anne-Marie nods and closes the door behind her

Poison my boy, my girl? Infect my home? Never. Not true. Never.

ACT II

Christmas Day. Early evening

The Christmas tree is in a corner. It's been stripped of its sweets, fruit and money, and the candles have been burnt down. Nora's overcoat lies on a chair

Nora is pacing the room. She listens towards the hall

Nora Who's there?

Anne-Marie enters from the hall, carrying a large cardboard box

Anne-Marie I found the costumes at last, right at the back of the ——
Nora Who was at the front door?
Anne-Marie No-one.
Nora I heard someone.
Anne-Marie On Christmas Day?
Nora I have to check the mail. (*She looks in to the hall; whispering to herself*) He couldn't ... Never ... My children.
Anne-Marie Mrs Nora?
Nora No letters.
Anne-Marie They're all looking a bit tattered.
Nora Oh, I could rip every single one to shreds!
Anne-Marie Heavens above, they're easy to mend.
Nora Yes. Kris can help me. I won't be long.
Anne-Marie Not again, Mrs Nora, you'll catch your death.
Nora Worse things have happened. Where are the children?
Anne-Marie Playing with their presents, poor lambs.
Nora They want to see me?
Anne-Marie They asked so politely.
Nora I won't be able to spend as much time with them from now on, Anne-Marie.
Anne-Marie Children can get used to almost anything.
Nora Would they remember me if I left and never came back?
Anne-Marie Heaven forbid.
Nora Anne-Marie. I've always wanted to ask. Your own daughter. How could you bear to give her up?

Anne-Marie I had to so I could become your nanny, little girl.

Nora But did you want that?

Anne-Marie I thanked my lucky stars. I was ruined, he was a good-for-nothing, he wasn't going to look after us. It was a job.

Nora Your daughter must have forgotten all about you.

Anne-Marie Heavens no. She wrote to me when she was confirmed, and when she got married.

Nora hugs her

Nora Anne-Marie. Dear old thing. You were such a good mother to me when I was little.

Anne-Marie The only mother you had, child.

Nora And if Ivor and Emmy ever found themselves on their own, I know you'd — no, no — (*she sorts through the box*) I'm busy, please, look in on them. There's so much to do. Tomorrow I have to stun the Stenborgs.

Anne-Marie There'll be no-one at the ball more beautiful than you, Mrs Nora.

She exits to Nora's room

Nora picks up her coat

Nora Out. Out. (*She throws down the coat and starts to unpack the box*) No-one here. Nothing can happen. (*She pulls out a single glove and searches for its matching pair*) What's the point of ...? Where's the matching ...? Forget, forget. Where on earth is the ...(*She screams. She starts for the door, but stops; uncertainly*) They're coming!

Kristine enters from the hall, having taken off her overcoat and scarf

Kristine. You.

Kristine Hallo, Nora.

Nora Are you on your own? I'm so glad you're here.

Kristine You left a message for me.

Nora Mmn, I was passing, because I need your help — sit, sit. The Stenborgs upstairs are having a fancy-dress party tomorrow night and Torvald's had an inspired idea, he wants me to go as a Neapolitan fishergirl and dance the tarantella, I learnt the tarantella in Capri.

Kristine In front of everyone? How spectacular.

Nora Yes. Torvald wants it. But look at the dress — you'd hardly know he had it made specially while we were down there, it's falling apart, what am I going to do?

Kristine It's just the hem. A few stitches. Needle and thread?

Kristine sews. Silence

Nora Thank you.
Kristine Thank you, Nora, for last night. A lovely evening.
Nora No, it wasn't a patch on the night before or the night before that, you should have come to town weeks ago. Torvald is quite the host.
Kristine Oh, a lot of it's down to you. You do your father proud. Is Dr Rank always so down in the mouth?
Nora He was worse than usual. He's very ill, consumption, his spine. His father had a lot of fun when he was alive — woman after woman, etcetera — it's poor Dr Rank who's paying for it. He's been ill since he was a boy. If you see what I mean.
Kristine You seem to know a lot about him?
Nora Pfff, you don't have to be a genius, I've got two children, haven't I, nurses and people drop in, things get said. All sorts of things get said.

Silence. Kristine sews

Kristine Does he come every day?
Nora (*nodding*) He's Torvald's oldest friend. And my friend. Part of the furniture.
Kristine Is he honest?
Nora Yes.
Kristine I wonder if he's a bit of a charmer?
Nora No.
Kristine Then why did he say mine was a familiar name in this house, when five seconds later your husband didn't have a clue who I was?
Nora Oh, Kris, Torvald's mad about me, that's all, just mad; he wants me, he wants to own every bit of me himself — he says that. He used to go green if I talked about my old friends from home, so I had to stop. But I can talk to Dr Rank about all that — he loves to listen.
Kristine Nora, don't take this the wrong way, but — I've got a few years on you, and you're such a child, really ... I think you need to find a way to get yourself out of this.
Nora Out of what?
Kristine This tangle with your rich admirer, the one you told me about ——
Nora I also told you he wasn't real, more's the pity.
Kristine Is Dr Rank wealthy?
Nora Yes.
Kristine No children?
Nora No ——

Kristine And he visits every day?

Nora Are you going deaf, Kris?

Kristine He's very pushy, isn't he, for a gentleman?

Nora What are you talking about?

Kristine I'm no genius, but obviously Dr Rank lent you the money.

Nora What a lunatic idea! How could you think that? Our friend, who visits every day? Yes, that would be a tangle.

Kristine So ...?

Nora No, no, no, didn't even occur to me. He wasn't even rich then. He inherited it later.

Kristine Oh. Well, lucky for you if you ask me, Nora.

Nora Not in a million years would I dream of asking — Though of course, if I were to, I'm sure he'd ——

Kristine But that would be a lunatic idea?

Nora Lunatic. Still, if I did have a quiet word in Dr Rank's ear ——

Kristine Behind Torvald's back?

Nora But don't you see it's all behind his back anyway? I have to get out of it, I have to find a way ...

Kristine Yes ...

Nora God, I wish I were a man. They're made for this.

Kristine We have our husbands for this.

Nora Pfff, drivel — that IOU, I need to get it back — once you've paid off your debt, you do, don't you, and then there's nothing to stop you ——

Kristine Nora ...

Nora Nothing to stop you from tearing the filthy thing into a thousand pieces!

Kristine Stop. What's happened? Something has.

Nora Why, can you read me? Is my face an open book!

Kristine Nora ——

Nora Kris — (*she hears something*) sshhh, Torvald. Play with the children. Take the sewing, he can't stand it. Find Anne-Marie. Please.

Kristine I'm not leaving this house till you've told me everything.

She exits to Nora's room. Torvald enters from the hall. He has a bundle of papers

Nora Torvald, home at last, safe and sound.

Torvald Was that the dressmaker?

Nora Kristine. She's helping me with my costume. And I will look perfect.

Torvald An inspired idea of mine, no?

Nora And very good of me to say yes.

Torvald Were you thinking of saying no? (*He takes her chin*) You didn't mean that, did you, squirrel? No, no. (*He makes to enter his study*) Carry on.

Nora Are you busy?
Torvald (*holding up the bundle of papers*) The bank, the bank.
Nora Torvald. (*He stops and raises his eyebrows*) Squirrel might need a
favour. Squirrel would ask for it so sweetly.
Torvald Mmn?
Nora Because then you couldn't say no, could you?
Torvald Depends.
Nora The lark would sing high sing low ...
Torvald She should change her tune, or she'll lose her voice.
Nora She'll turn into a fairy and do a moonlight dance.
Torvald Nora. This isn't this morning's favour, is it? Not again?
Nora Yes. Please.
Torvald You have the audacity ...? After everything I said?
Nora You have to do me this favour. You have to let Krogstad keep his job
at the bank.
Torvald Nora, it's his job I'm giving to Mrs Linde.
Nora That's lovely, thank you, but fire another junior, not Krogstad!
Torvald I don't believe this. You were wrong to make a promise to that man.
Because of that I have to ——
Nora But this is for you. Didn't you say he writes for those grubby papers?
—— he could hurt you, I'm scared, he terrifies me.
Torvald Nora. Ignore the ghosts.
Nora Ghosts?
Torvald Your father's case was nothing like ——
Nora Pa?
Torvald Isn't that what this is about?
Nora Yes. Remember what those monsters wrote about Pa? They'd have
sacked him, after those smears, if they hadn't sent you to look into it, if you
hadn't been so kind to him, and helpful.
Torvald Nora, your father was one kind of man. I'm nothing like him. I'm
a civil servant. I have a good name. I plan to keep it.
Nora But they're brutes, who knows what they could do? We're so happy,
Torvald, we nearly have everything — no worries in the world — Ivor and
Emmy; Torvald, please, I'm begging you ——
Torvald And that's what makes it impossible. My colleagues know he's
about to be sacked. If they hear I've changed my mind because of my little
wife ——
Nora So what?
Torvald Stop being so hot-headed: I can't let you have your way. I'd be
laughed out of the building. Do you want everyone to think I buckle under
the slightest pressure? I'd pay for that. Dearly. Anyway, I'm firing
Krogstad for more than one reason.
Nora Oh?

Torvald Bad character's one thing, I could ignore it if I had to ——
Nora *Yes, yes, you could.*
Torvald I even hear he's not a bad worker. But he and I go back too far. We were friends as students. Just one of those things — and very irritating now. He thinks he has the right to call me Torvald, Nora. In front of others. I can't stand the man's backslapping; it makes me blush to think about it. We're not on first-name terms. He can't stay at the bank, he'd undermine me.
Nora You can't mean that?
Torvald What did you say?
Nora That's all so — petty.
Torvald You think I'm ——?
Nora Of course I don't, Torvald, that's why I'm so surprised ——
Torvald You think this is petty, so you think I'm petty? Petty! (*He calls*) Anne-Marie! (*To Nora*) Enough. (*He rummages through his papers*)
Nora What are you doing?

Anne-Marie enters

Torvald Go out and find a boy to deliver this letter straight away. (*He gives Anne-Marie an envelope and some money*)
Anne-Marie Yes, sir.

She exits

Torvald The dye's cast. Hot-headed child.
Nora Torvald, what was that?
Torvald Krogstad's notice.
Nora Get it back, stop her, you have to for your own good, or do it for me, for our children. For God's sake, Torvald, call the letter back you have no idea what it's going to do to us.
Torvald Too late.

A wild intake of breath from Nora as she stares after Anne-Marie

All this fear, Nora? I won't hold it against you, but it's an insult. Yes, an insult. Yes. You think I should give in because a seedy hack with a grudge might retaliate? I'll overlook it, because you love me. You love me. And I can't hold that against you, can I? (*He takes her in his arms*) Priceless girl. You know the way of things. What will be, will be, Nora. And when we're up against it, if there's a real crisis, I'll be man enough for it.
Nora For what?
Torvald Anything.
Nora You'll never have to face that. Never.

Torvald We'll do it together then, man and wife. That's the way. (*He caresses her*) Smile, giddy girl. Everything's all right. Now, the tarantella! Where's your tambourine? Be as loud as you like, I won't hear a thing. Rank knows where to find me.

He gathers his papers and exits to his study, closing the door behind him

Nora stands stock still

Nora He can do it. "What will be?" Never. Get out of it. Somehow.

The doorbell rings

Anything. Dr Rank. Dr Rank? (*She composes herself and opens the door to the hall*)

Dr Rank is in the hallway, hanging up his coat

During the following it begins to grow dark

Dr Rank; no, no, in here. Torvald's busy.
Dr Rank And you're not?
Nora I've time enough for you.
Dr Rank I'll make use of that then, Mrs Helmer. Whatever you can spare me.
Nora What's that supposed to mean?
Dr Rank Well, time's running out.
Nora (*shaking her head*) But ——
Dr Rank I know. Does the clock really have to tick-tick so fast?
Nora (*grabbing his arm*) What do you know? Tell me.
Dr Rank I'm done for.
Nora Oh, you mean you.
Dr Rank Who else? Patient: Rank. Top of my own critical list. I've looked inside, taken stock, and I'm broke. Who knows, by February I might be graveyard bones.
Nora Revolting talk.
Dr Rank Well, it is revolting. One last examination, and I'll know how long I've got before I start to break apart. Now, listen to me. About Helmer. He's sensitive, he can't stand ... Well, he couldn't stand this. I don't want him anywhere near me.
Nora Dr Rank ——
Dr Rank No, he's to stay away. I'll bar the door. As soon as I know, I'll send you my card with a black cross struck through it. That'll be your sign. This filthy body will be on the verge of giving up the ghost.

Nora Well aren't you a gloomy foghorn today? Just when I wanted you to be in a good mood.

Dr Rank Blame my father. Rough justice, isn't it, that I have to die because he liked to sin? Still, in every family someone gets what should have gone to someone else.

Nora Shut up! Be happy! Laugh!

Dr Rank Quite right, let's make a joke of it. My skeleton moulders because Rank Senior, Second Lieutenant, danced his youth away. Ha!

Nora He loved his asparagus, didn't he, your pa? And pâté de foie gras?

Dr Rank Yes, and truffles.

Nora That's right, truffles. And oysters, too?

Dr Rank Oysters, definitely, oysters.

Nora And port, and champagne. All so — delicious. It's a tragedy, the things those delights can do to a skeleton.

Dr Rank Yes, especially if the skeleton in question has never even had a pinch of pleasure from them.

Nora Oh, that's the biggest tragedy of all.

Dr Rank regards her. Silence

Why did you smile?

Dr Rank You laughed.

Nora No, you smiled.

Dr Rank You're a scoundrel. A thoroughbred scoundrel.

Nora How thrilling to do something absolutely mad.

Dr Rank Today could be the day.

Nora (*putting her hands on his shoulders*) You'll never die, Dr Rank. You'll always be alive to Torvald and me.

Dr Rank Out of sight, out of mind.

Nora Do you think so?

Dr Rank New friends come along, sure as death and taxes.

Nora Sure as that?

Dr Rank Look at Mrs Linde.

Nora Kris? You green-eyed monster.

Dr Rank She'll replace me, I know that.

Nora Sshh, she's in there.

Dr Rank And so it begins.

Nora She's mending my costume! Good God, you foghorn, pipe down. Be nice, Dr Rank. Because tomorrow, I'm a Neapolitan. And when I dance, know this: it's for you. And Torvald, of course, but also — for ... (*She takes a few items from the box*) Sit.

Dr Rank sits

What do you think?

Dr Rank What is it?

Nora What do you think?

Dr Rank Stockings. Silk.

Nora The colour of flesh. Gorgeous. It's too dark in here, but tomorrow you'll see how — no, only the foot. All right, a little bit more.

Dr Rank Hmn.

Nora Why such a face? Don't you think they'll fit?

Dr Rank I could never have a point of view on that.

Silence

Nora Shameful. (*She flicks him lightly on the ear with the stockings*) Take that. (*She puts them away*)

Dr Rank Any more treasures?

Nora Not a nugget for you, because you're very very bad. (*She hums as she hunts through the box. Silence*)

Dr Rank I wonder — sitting here with you — this close — what in God's name would have happened to me if I'd never come to this house?

Nora One of us. Family.

Dr Rank Not for long.

Nora Shush. Always.

Dr Rank Yet I won't even find a way to leave a thank you. Nothing will stay of me, not even a footprint.

Nora Dr Rank?

Dr Rank Yes?

Nora If I asked — for you to give me some token …

Dr Rank Name it.

Nora This would be a big favour …

Dr Rank Could you really make me that happy at last?

Nora You don't have a clue what I'm talking about, yet.

Dr Rank I'm listening.

Nora I can't. It's not just a favour, it's much more than that. It's huge.

Dr Rank Name it. Please. Don't you trust me?

Nora More than anyone. You're a true friend. All right, Dr Rank. You have to help me stop something. You know how much Torvald loves me, there isn't a thing he wouldn't do for me, he'd die for me.

Dr Rank Do you think he's the only man who feels like that, Nora?

This is a shock to her. She controls it

Is he the only man who'd give his life for you?

She understands, and she sighs sadly

I swore I'd tell you before my time was up. Now or never. Yes, Nora. My God, you can trust me now. I'll do anything, anything.

Nora Let me pass.

Dr Rank Nora.

Nora Anne-Marie, the lamp! That was wrong, Dr Rank.

Dr Rank Wrong that I love you?

Nora Wrong to tell me. You really didn't need to.

Dr Rank You mean you knew?

Anne-Marie enters with the lamp, puts it down, and exits

Nora? Mrs Helmer —? Did you —?

Nora Oh, who knows what I knew and didn't? Clumsy. Everything was perfect the way it was.

Dr Rank Well there you have it. I'm yours. Tell me what you need, for God's sake ...

Nora looks him in the eye and shakes her head resolutely

Don't torture me.

Nora Not now. Not after that. I don't need help anyway, it's all up here, I made it all up.

Silence. She smiles at him

Well aren't you a card, Dr Rank? It's light in here now, you should be as red as the king of diamonds.

Dr Rank But I'm not embarrassed by anything. Will I leave and not come back?

Nora Don't be silly, Torvald needs you, nothing changes.

Dr Rank And you?

Nora I always have lots of fun when you're here.

Dr Rank Ah, and so she baffles me yet again. Strange girl. I often wonder if you enjoy my company more than Helmer's.

Nora There are people you love. And people you like to be with. And sometimes ...

Dr Rank Yes.

Nora I loved Papa. He was my favourite, of course. But at the same time, I loved to creep downstairs to be with the maids. They didn't tell me what to do, it was great fun down there.

Dr Rank I've succeeded them, then?

Nora You know I didn't mean that, Dr Rank. But — do you see? — I suppose Torvald is a bit like Pa ...

Anne-Marie enters from the hall

Anne-Marie Mrs Helmer?

She whispers to Nora and hands her a visiting card. Nora looks at it, doesn't quite hide her agitation and puts it in her pocket

Dr Rank Is something the matter?
Nora My costume's arrived.
Dr Rank I thought Mrs Linde was mending your ——
Nora Another one, bought specially, a surprise.
Dr Rank Ah, so that's the huge secret?
Nora Go in and see him, keep him busy, keep him out.
Dr Rank You're safe. He'll have to get through me first.

He exits to Torvald's study

Nora The kitchen?
Anne-Marie He came to the back door!
Nora Did you tell him I was busy?
Anne-Marie It didn't do any good, he won't leave till he's spoken to you.
Nora All right. Don't tell anyone. It's a surprise for Torvald.

Anne-Marie nods and exits

(*Whispering*) Something terrifying? Something ——? Never.

She locks the door to Torvald's study

Anne-Marie brings Krogstad into the room, then retires. Krogstad is dressed for travelling: fur coat, galoshes, fur hat

Nora Keep your voice down: my husband's at home.
Krogstad It makes no difference.
Nora What do you want?
Krogstad I've been fired. It can't be news to you.
Nora There was nothing I could do, Mr Krogstad. I tried, I tried.
Krogstad Then he can't love you very much. When he knows I've got you in the palm of my hand ——
Nora What makes you think he knows?
Krogstad Ah. The idea that Torvald had found his manhood seemed a bit far-fetched.
Nora Helmer to you, who do you think you are!

Krogstad Oh, I'll remember to call him Mr Helmer — when it's appropriate. Whisper, whisper. I wonder: are you finally beginning to realize how serious this is?

Nora What do you want?

Krogstad To see you, that's all. I haven't stopped thinking about you. Yes, Mrs Helmer, debt-collectors feel. The hack has a heart.

Nora Then think of my children.

Krogstad Have you or your husband thought of mine? It doesn't matter, you don't need to panic. I wanted to tell you I'm not going to do anything, not yet.

Nora Yes, that's right, I knew you wouldn't …

Krogstad No-one else need know. We can find a way through this, the three of us.

Nora My husband can't know.

Krogstad What can you do? Can you pay the debt?

Nora Not straight away.

Krogstad Can you raise the money in the next few days?

Nora Not by proper means.

Krogstad Even if you could it wouldn't do you a scrap of good. Offer me all the cash in the world, I won't give you your IOU back.

Nora Why?

Krogstad It needs to be kept safe. I'm not going to tell anyone. So if you're thinking of doing something drastic ——

Nora I am.

Krogstad — disappearing ——

Nora I will.

Krogstad — or something more decisive ——

Nora Yes.

Krogstad — forget it.

Nora How did you know?

Krogstad It's not a particularly original thought. God knows I didn't have what it takes.

Nora I ——

Krogstad And you don't either.

Nora I — (*She shakes her head*)

Krogstad Anyway, it'd be stupid. After the scandal died down, I'd simply send your husband the letter in my pocket ——

Nora shakes her head

— it explains everything, without the grisly detail.

Nora He mustn't see it, rip it up, I'll get the money.

Krogstad Listen, I've already told you ——

Nora I'm not talking about what I owe you. Tell me how much you want
from him, I'll get it.

Krogstad I don't want money from Torvald Helmer! I want my life back.

Nora stares

I want to stand tall again. And he's going to help me, Mrs Helmer. I'm not
bad. I've done nothing wrong for two years; I've worked every day at that
bank. I've struggled, but it was all I ever wanted: to work my way up, rung
by rung. And now? Elbowed off again. Reinstatement isn't enough. I want
a promotion. To the new position Torvald's going to create for me.

Nora You're dreaming.

Krogstad I know him. As long as things are seemly. I'll go back, and you
watch. In a year, he'll be answering to me. Manager: Krogstad. That
position will be mine, not Torvald Helmer's.

Nora They'll dance on your grave before that happens.

Krogstad Or I'll dance on yours?

Nora I'll do it, I've got what it takes ——

Krogstad You're very soft, and very spoiled, and you don't scare me.

Nora You wait.

Krogstad Push yourself through the ice? Deep into the black, bitter water?
Till some poor child sees you floating by in spring, putrefied, bald ——?

Nora I'm not scared of you.

Krogstad Nor I of you. People don't do it, Mrs Helmer. And what'd be the
point? I've got Torvald where I want him.

Nora Even after I'm dead?

Krogstad You mean when I have my finger on your memory?

Nora stares at him, speechless

Don't be stupid. I look forward to hearing from Torvald, once he gets this.
(*He takes the letter from his pocket*) And never forget: he made me do it.
He forced this out of me. I'll never forgive him.

He exits through the hall

Nora runs to the door, inches it open and listens

Nora He won't. He can't.

*Silence. Perhaps it won't happen. A letter falls into the letter-box. Nora stifles
a scream. Krogstad's footsteps diminish. She approaches the letter-box——*

... Torvald ... Torvald ... Torvald ...

Kristine enters from Nora's room with the dress

Kristine You can try it on now. Nora?
Nora Kris. Kris. The letter-box. Through the glass. See?
Kristine — yes?
Nora From Krogstad. Locked inside.
Kristine Nora? Krogstad lent you the money!
Nora Torvald's about to find out.
Kristine Nora — this is for the best, I know it, I know it.
Nora You don't know the half of it. I forged my father's signature ——
Kristine What?
Nora — no let me say this first: you're here, Kris, you can see me, and hear me, you'll tell them ——
Kristine Tell them —?
Nora If I go mad — and I could ——
Kristine Nora!
Nora — or if something happens, if I'm not here ——
Kristine Get a hold of yourself ——
Nora — if someone has to take the blame, then you were here with me now, so you'll tell them ——
Kristine Nora ...
Nora — that I wasn't mad today, that I'm sane, that no-one else knew about this, no-one. It was me, all of it. Yes?
Kristine Yes. But I don't understand.
Nora You couldn't. Something's about to happen. The — wondrous — miraculous something ...
Kristine Miraculous —?
Nora A miraculous thing. But it's terrifying, Kris. It can't happen, not for all the world.
Kristine I'll go and talk to Krogstad.
Nora He'll hurt you.
Kristine No. I know the man, Nora. He'd have done anything for me, once.

Nora stares

Where does he live?
Nora I don't ... (*She gives her Krogstad's visiting card*) But the letter!

Torvald knocks on the door and calls from his study

Torvald (*off*) Nora!

Nora screams

Nora Hallo — you can't come in yet!

Torvald (*off*) All right, don't panic. You've locked the door — and I've got no idea that you're trying on your costume.

Nora That's right — I'm going to look stunning!

Kristine has read the card

Kristine It's not far.

Nora What's the use? We're done for. The letter.

Kristine Torvald has the key?

Nora The only one.

Kristine Krogstad will have to demand it back unopened. Any excuse he can think of.

Nora But the time — Torvald always checks the ——

Kristine Do something. Distract him. I'll be as quick as I can.

She rushes off via the hall

Nora approaches Torvald's door, unlocks it and peeps in

Nora Torvald?

Torvald (*off*) So the man of the house is finally allowed in his own living ——

Torvald enters, followed by Dr Rank

Oh. You talk too much, Rank. I thought we were in for a treat?

Dr Rank So did I. Obviously I had it wrong.

Nora You'll all get to see me in my glory tomorrow, and not before.

Torvald You look worn out, Nora. Too much rehearsal?

Nora I haven't rehearsed at all.

Torvald You'll need to.

Nora I know, Torvald, but how can I without you? I've forgotten everything.

Torvald We'll soon brush you up.

Nora Yes. That's right, I need your help, Torvald. Now. I'm so worried. The grand party. Yes, tonight, you have to devote yourself to me ——

Torvald All right, Nora.

Nora — pen down ——

Torvald All yours, sweet lark.

Nora — no work, all evening.

Torvald All evening. (*He approaches the hall*)

Nora No, Torvald!

Torvald Nora. Enough. (*He makes to go*)

Nora rushes to the piano and plays the opening bars of the tarantella

Torvald stops

Nora I will never dance tomorrow if we don't rehearse today.

Torvald turns and smiles

There's no time like the present, is there? Dinner's not ready. Play for me, Torvald. You have to teach me. You know everything. You've got to be here for me, always.
Torvald Are you really that nervous?
Nora You've no idea. Teach me.
Torvald Well, if that's what you want. Why not? (*He sits at the piano*)

Norah grabs the tambourine and a long multi-coloured shawl from the cardboard box. She whirls the shawl around her shoulders and springs to the floor

Nora Play. Play.

Torvald plays. Nora dances. Dr Rank watches

Torvald (*as he plays*) Slower …
Nora I don't understand that, faster!
Torvald Too violent, Nora …
Nora But this is the way!

Torvald stops playing

Torvald No, no. Hopeless.
Nora (*laughing; swinging her tambourine*) What did I tell you?
Dr Rank Let me play for her.
Torvald Yes. That was madness. Don't you remember anything? We'll try again. Now, begin.

Dr Rank sits at the piano and plays. Nora dances, ferociously. Torvald tries to correct her during this but she doesn't seem to hear. Her hair flies loose and falls over her shoulders. She dances and dances

Kristine enters. She stands still in the doorway

Nora Kris, Kris, look at me!
Torvald But you're dancing as if your life depended on it.
Nora It does.

Torvald Stop! Stop! Rank, enough!

Dr Rank stops playing. Nora stops dancing suddenly

I don't believe this. You've forgotten everything I ever taught you.

Nora (*throws the tambourine down*) Didn't I say?

Torvald We'll need to start from scratch.

Nora Yes, definitely. I'm hopeless, Torvald, and if you don't teach me, I'll fail.

Torvald That won't happen, I promise you.

Nora No-one but me today and tomorrow. No-one but Nora. No work, no friends, no letters.

Torvald There's a letter out there, isn't there? From Krogstad?

Nora I couldn't say, I think so, but forget him, forget all about him.

Torvald You're not still scared of that man ...?

Nora No yes no yes no reading no letters nothing terrible can happen to us not till it's all over nothing not now.

Dr Rank (*to Torvald; sotto voce*) I'd take her at her word, if I were you.

Torvald (*putting his arm around her*) You'll have your way today, giddy girl. But tomorrow after you've danced ——

Nora Then you'll be free.

Anne-Marie enters

Anne-Marie Dinner is ready, Mrs Helmer.

Nora Champagne glasses on the table, Anne-Marie — for champagne!

Anne-Marie nods and exits

Torvald Oh, I see, a party?

Nora Yes, we're going to make merry till day-break! (*She shouts*) And macaroons for once, Anne-Marie, bags and bags of them!

Torvald (*taking her hands*) Nora Lark. Where have you gone? Are you there?

Nora I'm here. Always. Go through, Torvald. Dr Rank. Kristine has to help me with my hair.

Dr Rank and Torvald start to leave. The following is spoken sotto voce

Dr Rank Is she — perhaps (*whispering*) — um — in a certain condition?

Torvald No, no. Fear, as I said. Girlish fear.

They exit

Nora Well?

Kristine Gone to the country.

Nora I knew it.

Kristine He's back tomorrow night; I've left a message.

Nora You needn't have bothered. Don't try to stop anything. In a way, it makes me happy, just to wait here for the something — the miraculous something ...

Kristine What are you waiting for?

Nora You wouldn't understand. Go in, Kris. I'm coming.

Kristine exits

Nora collects herself. She looks at her watch

Midnight in seven hours. Twenty-four hours after that, the tarantella will be done. Twenty-four plus seven. Thirty-one hours of life.

Torvald appears in the doorway

Torvald Lark? Lark, where are you?

Nora (*rushing towards him with arms open wide*) Here. Here. Here is your lark!

ACT III

Boxing Day. Evening

The lamp is lit. Dance music can be heard from the floor above

Kristine is ushering Krogstad in from the hall

Kristine Thank you for coming.

Krogstad A message from you? Of all people?

Kristine We need to talk.

Krogstad About what, for God's sake? And why here?

Kristine I don't know anyone else. You couldn't come to me, my landlady never takes her eyes off the front door. I knew we'd be alone. The Helmers are upstairs at a party.

Krogstad Are they? Drinking and dancing? Tonight?

Kristine Is there something wrong with that?

Krogstad Honestly, it makes no difference to me.

Kristine We don't have much time.

Krogstad Well then, Mrs Linde, I suppose you'd better get on with it.

Kristine Kristine, Nils. Please call me Kristine.

Krogstad Mrs Linde, I'm confused.

Kristine Yes, well, you've never understood me, have you?

Krogstad Oh, I understood. It wasn't very complicated. A cold-blooded woman threw a man away because she got a better offer. The oldest story in the book.

Kristine Stop it. Please stop. You don't think I found leaving you easy? You couldn't think that?

Krogstad Given what you wrote me, yes.

Kristine I had to write that letter. I had to leave you. So it felt right to choke dead everything you felt for me. Somehow that seemed more honest.

Krogstad Here's honesty for you: he was rich, I wasn't.

Kristine My mother, Mr Krogstad. My brothers. She was so frail, they were young; and things didn't look very promising for you then, did they? Honestly, could you have supported us?

Krogstad I don't know.

Kristine We had to live.

Krogstad You had no right to do what you did to me!

Silence

Kristine, you broke me. My world gave way. I lost everything. You had no right.

Kristine I don't know. I've never known.

Silence

Krogstad Why are you here?

Kristine Things can change.

Krogstad They were about to, then you got in the way.

Kristine I had no idea I'd be taking your job at the bank, Nils.

Krogstad Yes; but will you turn it down?

Kristine It wouldn't do you a speck of good.

Krogstad Say no anyway.

Kristine That wouldn't make any sense.

Krogstad For God's sake, what are you trying to do?

Kristine Please, there isn't much time, hear me out. Nils, you know why I'm here. You must. My life isn't so different from yours. I'm on my own now. Couldn't we start again?

Krogstad What?

Kristine Couldn't we?

Krogstad Us?

Kristine I'm not here for a job. Of course I have to work, work's the only thing that makes real sense, but what's the point when I feel so useless and lonely? I'm here for you, Nils. It's me. It's Kristine.

Krogstad I don't believe this: you're hysterical.

Kristine You know me better than that.

Krogstad Do you know what's happened to me?

Kristine Yes.

Krogstad Everything?

Kristine Yes.

Krogstad (*pointing outside*) I'm a pariah, to them out there.

Kristine If we'd stayed together, who knows? It would have all been different.

Krogstad I'm certain of that.

Kristine It could still happen.

Krogstad Kristine, do you know what you're saying?

Kristine I think we could be happy.

Krogstad You really have what it takes to walk out there — with me?

Kristine You've got children. I need to be a mother. And we need each other. I've always seen the man inside. Yes, I have what it takes. I'd do anything.

She approaches him. They clasp hands

Krogstad Kristine! (*He suddenly detaches himself*)

Kristine listens towards the ceiling

Oh, God. You don't know what I've done.
Kristine Huh, the tarantella! Quickly, they'll be back any second.
Krogstad Kristine, it's hopeless. You don't know what I've done to the
Helmers ——
Kristine Yes, I do know.
Krogstad And you still want me?
Kristine For God's sake, I understand you were driven to it. In any case, Nils,
your letter's still in the box.
Krogstad What?
Kristine Yes!

Krogstad stares at her

Krogstad Ah. I see. This is about her, isn't it? You'd do whatever it takes
to rescue her, wouldn't you, Kristine? Out with it. Be honest with me.
Kristine I sold my heart for the sake of others once. I'd rather die than do
it twice.
Krogstad I'll demand my letter back ——

Kristine shakes her head

— I'll tell Helmer it's nothing, a childish complaint about my sacking, he
can't read it.
Kristine No. Don't do that.
Krogstad But your friend — isn't that the real reason you asked me to meet
you here?
Kristine Yes. But that was yesterday: I panicked. Now, well … It has to
come out. Torvald has to know. This secret is disastrous for them. They
have to see the truth about each other.
Krogstad No more lies. If you say so. There's one thing I *can* do though and
I'll do it now.
Kristine The tarantella's over, you have to leave! No, use the back door or
they'll see you — the housekeeper's asleep.
Krogstad I'll be on Olsen Street.
Kristine We can walk home together.
Krogstad Kristine.
Kristine A new beginning.
Krogstad Thank you.
Kristine The world's a surprise, isn't it, Nils?
Krogstad You've made me so happy.

He exits

Torvald's and Nora's voices are heard outside

Kristine can hardly contain her happiness. She puts on her hat and coat

A key is turned and Torvald leads Nora into the hall, almost by force. She's dressed in the Italian costume with a large black shawl draped over her shoulders. He's wearing evening dress with a big black cloak. Nora resists entering the living-room

Nora No, back, back — why leave so early?
Torvald Nora — hurry, it's freezing.
Nora Please, please, another hour.
Torvald Not another minute. Our agreement. (*He pulls her into the room*)
Kristine Good-evening.
Nora Kris!
Torvald Mrs Linde? It's past your bed-time, isn't it?
Kristine I'm sorry, I so wanted to see Nora all dressed up. You'd left by the time I arrived, I just had to wait.
Torvald (*pulling off Nora's shawl*) Worth it, no?
Kristine Beautiful.
Torvald Ravishing. Stunning. So said every Stenborg. But the giddy girl's got a very hot head. I almost had to twist her arm off.
Nora You'll be sorry you didn't let me stay another half hour, Torvald.
Torvald Hear that, Mrs Linde? She dances her tarantella — she's the belle of the ball — even if she is a tad artless, even if the dance has the odd, let's say, embellishment, that isn't strictly authentic. But who cares? — she charms, she stuns, and she has no idea when to make an exit. Curtain, Capri girl! So I take her arm, one last turn around the room, a nod to our hosts, and then, like a princess in a fairy-story, she vanishes. Drama, Mrs Linde. She'll never get it. Why is it so hot in here? (*He throws his cloak down and opens the door to his study*) And dark in here?

Torvald exits to his study to light some candles

Nora Well?
Kristine I've spoken to him.
Nora And?
Kristine Nora, you have to tell Torvald everything.
Nora I knew it.
Kristine No, you're safe from Krogstad, but still: tell Torvald everything.

Nora shakes her head resolutely

Then the letter will.

Nora You're my dearest friend, Kris. Thank you. I know what to do now.

Torvald returns

Torvald So, Mrs Linde, have you looked her over?
Kristine Yes. Good-night.
Torvald Off already? Don't forget your knitting.
Kristine Oh. Thank you.
Torvald Not a patch on embroidery, by the way.
Kristine Oh?
Torvald Embroidery: elegant. Left hand like so, needle with the right. Harmony.
Kristine Erm, yes.
Torvald Knitting: chaos. Clanking needles, flapping wrists. Much too Chinese. Now that was good champagne.
Kristine Well. Good-night, Nora. Think, for once. Think.
Torvald Quite right, Mrs Linde.
Kristine Good-night, Mr Helmer.
Torvald Night-night. You know your way? I'd accompany you, but it isn't that far, is it?

Kristine exits

Torvald closes the door behind her

Do we tell the town bore he has a rival? I thought we'd never see the back of her.
Nora You must be tired.
Torvald Not in the slightest. You?
Nora Yes. Sleep soon.
Torvald I was right to bring you home.
Nora You're always right, Torvald.
Torvald (*kisses her forehead*) Good girl. Clever lark for saying so. Wasn't Rank on good form this evening?
Nora I didn't get a chance to speak to him.
Torvald Neither did I, really, but for the first time in ages he seemed on top of the world.

Silence. He stares at her

Home at last. Just we two.
Nora Don't look at me like that.
Torvald My own priceless find. All mine. Every part of you.

Nora Not tonight, please.

Torvald Ah, still the fishergirl? The tarantella, raging about inside? Hot blood. Hmn. The guests are leaving. Hush-hush. And then it'll be silent.

Nora Silent, yes.

Torvald You knew I was playing the game didn't you, at the party? You know the game, don't you, Nora? You're my secret lover. A stolen glance. Another. Sshh. Because no-one knows.

Nora Yes, I realize you never stop thinking about me.

Torvald And by the time we leave, you're my bride. I throw the shawl over your shoulders; slide my fingers across this long neck; we walk home together; our first time, your lips tremble. Ravishing. Temptress. God, you sent me wild up there — I couldn't hold on, why do you think I wanted to come home so early?

Nora Go away, Torvald, not now, I don't want this.

Torvald Tease, Nora, you're *mine*. My *wife*.

A knock on the front door

Nora starts. Torvald shouts towards the hall

Yes?

Dr Rank (*off*) Only me. Can I come in for a second?

Torvald What the hell does he want?

Torvald opens the door to the hall

Dr Rank enters

Very kind of you not to walk straight past, Rank.

Dr Rank Helmer, Helmer, Helmer. How could I leave without stopping by my second home?

Torvald You seemed home enough upstairs.

Dr Rank Yes, a wonderful evening, and what of it? We should all try everything, shouldn't we? Cling to life. How was the champagne for you?

Torvald The best I've tasted all year.

Dr Rank I agree. Lost count of how many glasses I managed to wash down.

Nora So did Torvald.

Dr Rank Hmn?

Nora Merry Torvald.

Dr Rank A man should have a bit of fun after a good long day.

Torvald Unfortunately I can't pat myself on the back for that.

Dr Rank Fortunately, I can. (*He slaps his back*)

Nora Today, Dr Rank? Your last, um, scientific examination?

Dr Rank Yes. Today.
Torvald "Scientific examination"! Such big words, little Nora!
Nora Good news, I hope?
Dr Rank Yes, the best possible news, for doctor and patient. Certainity.
Nora (*quickly and searchingly*) Certainity?
Dr Rank Utter certainity. So why shouldn't I down a little champagne?
Nora Yes, Dr Rank, you deserved it.
Torvald You'll pay for it in the morning, though.
Dr Rank You don't get something for nothing in this world.
Nora Dr Rank, what about the next fancy-dress party? I think we should decide on our theme.
Torvald How many balls, little Nora, do you need to be belle of?
Dr Rank You will go as Fortuna, goddess of good-luck.
Torvald We'll need some, to find a costume for that.
Dr Rank She won't need one. She only need go as herself.
Torvald Charming thought. You old flatterer. And what will you go as?
Dr Rank An invisible man.
Torvald That's a bit eccentric, isn't it? — even for you.
Dr Rank I'll find the Big Black Invisible Hat, I'll pull it over my ears, and no-one will even know I'm there.

Torvald contains a nervous laugh

Now give me what I came for, Helmer. One of those cigars of yours. A black Havana.
Torvald With pleasure.

Torvald offers him the box. Dr Rank takes a cigar and cuts off the end

Thank you.

Nora strikes a match

A-ha! Fire.

She lights his cigar

Thanks. Now goodbye.
Torvald Goodbye, old man.
Nora Sweet dreams, Dr Rank.
Dr Rank Thank you.
Nora Wish me the same.
Dr Rank Sweet dreams, Nora Helmer. Many thanks.

Dr Rank nods to them both and exits

Silence

Torvald You see? On top of the world.
Nora Yes.

Torvald takes out his keys and goes into the hall

Where are you going?
Torvald Tomorrow's papers won't fit inside that letter-box if I don't empty it now.
Nora You'll be working tonight?
Torvald The last thing on my mind. As if you didn't know. (*At the letter-box*) Hmn. Who's been picking at ——
Nora At what?
Torvald Has Anne-Marie —? (*He finds a hairpin. He holds it out to Nora*) Is this hair-pin yours?
Nora Those children.
Torvald Tell them they mustn't do it again. (*He takes the letters out*) Anne-Marie, put the lamp out out here! (*He comes back into the living-room, leafing through a pile of letters. He stops*)
Nora (*whispering*) No, Torvald.
Torvald Hallo? Rank's card.Two. Odd.
Nora What do they say?
Torvald Nothing. There's a black cross over his name. (*He holds one up to her*) How morbid, is it some kind of death notice?
Nora Yes.
Torvald What? Do you know something?
Nora It's his goodbye to us. Now, he'll lock the world out, and die.
Torvald Oh ... Oh, the poor old boy. I knew of course, but I had no idea it would happen so quickly. I thought he'd be mine for — Why is he hiding himself away like some bleeding animal?
Nora Sometimes there's no need for words is there, Torvald?
Torvald Rank. How could he not be here? He's a part of us. Lonely man. All that pain. He's always made me feel grateful. There was his life, and there was ours, so different. Poor soul. Perhaps this is right. No more words. Right for him. (*He puts his arms around her*) And maybe for us, Nora. No one else now. I just want to press your head into my neck; God, it's insane, sometimes I wish you were inches from death, just so I could put it all on the line to save you.
Nora (*detaching herself*) Read your letters, Torvald.
Torvald No you, *you*, I want —

Nora Dr Rank, your friend, *Dr Rank.*

Torvald Yes. Too much death. Too much ugliness. You're right. We have to forget. I'll sleep in my own room tonight. Good night. Sweet dreams.

Torvald makes for his study with the letters. She throws her arms around his neck

  Good-night, Torvald. Good-night!

Torvald (*kissing her forehead*) My lark. I won't be long.

He takes the letters into his study and closes the door

Nora, despairing, fumbles about, finds Torvald's cloak and throws it over her shoulders

Nora Will never see him. (*She throws the black shawl over her head*) Nor my children. Never. The black water. Torvald. Ivor. Emmy. Huh! (*Somehow she knows he's discovered it. She stares ahead. And then it's over*) Goodbye.

She is about to rush out through the hall

  Torvald throws open his door and stands there with an open letter in his hand

Torvald Nora.

Nora screams

  What — what is — do you know what this says?

Nora Yes. Let me out.

Torvald (*holds her back*) Where are you going?

Nora (*tries to tear herself away*) No, Torvald, don't try to save me.

Torvald But it's not true? No — how could it be —?

Nora Yes. It's true. I loved you more than I loved anything.

Torvald Stop — don't — *twitter* ...

Nora Torvald ——

Torvald You pitiful ... Don't move. What have you done? What have you done?

Nora Let me out, don't take it on yourself, not for me.

Torvald Stop it ... Stop — *acting.* (*He blocks the doorway*) Do you understand what you've done? Answer! Do you see?

Nora stares at him. There's a coldness about her

Nora Yes. I'm beginning to see everything.

Torvald Good God. You? I've been asleep. I've been fast asleep. *You.* A hypocrite? A liar? And a criminal? Disgusting. Shame.

Nora stares at him, unblinking. He faces her

Oh, but I should have known. Clear as day. That father of yours was a filthy, reckless — shut your mouth. Immoral, no sense of duty, no love of God. Just like him, aren't you? I had it coming — stepping in back then to help him, when I *knew* — for you. You pay me back like this?

Nora Like this.

Torvald Everything's gone, you realize that, hmn? And *you've* done this to *me*? You've demolished me? I can't take it in. That man's dead inside. I'm at his mercy. He's a thug, he can do what he likes, I'm his. On my knees, because of a filthy woman.

Nora When I'm gone from the world, you'll be free.

Torvald Oh, be quiet. Stop posturing. You're worse than your father. How would it help me if you "went from the world"? Krogstad can still shout my shame from the rooftops. And, my God, what's to stop everyone thinking I was a conspirator? Thank you, Nora, thank you. When I've nestled you here in the palm of this hand every day since our wedding. I don't think you understand at all. Look what you've done to me. Can you *see*?

Nora Yes, I can.

Torvald Right, we'll have to take care of it. Take off that shawl. Take it off! I'll have to keep him happy — pay. And keep a lid on it. Never breathe a word. Got that? I'll save our faces even if it bankrupts us. You'll stay put of course, and no-one will know. But in here — in here — you're never to go near the children. I can't trust you with them now. Dear God, how could you drive me to this? I loved you, I still love … (*He shakes his head*) No, that's over. There's nothing left. Nothing except — this.

The doorbell rings. Torvald starts

Christ. He couldn't —— ? Hide, Nora. Say you're ill.

Nora stands stock still. Torvald opens the door to the hall

Anne-Marie is there, half-dressed. She holds out a letter to Torvald

Anne-Marie For Mrs Helmer.

Torvald snatches it and closes the door

Anne-Marie retires

Torvald Stay where you are. (*He looks at the front of the letter for confirmation. He nods*)
Nora You read it.
Torvald (*pauses*) Dear God ... (*He can't stand it any longer and tears the letter open. He scans it. He establishes that there's an accompanying document. A cry of joy*) Nora.

Nora stares at him. He reads it again, nodding

Yes ... Yes ... I'm saved. Nora, I'm saved.
Nora And me?
Torvald You too, of course, both of us, look, look: your IOU. Says he's sorry — takes it back — some bolt from the blue, it's changed his ... Oh, who gives a damn, we're saved. No-one can hurt you. No-one ... (*He looks at the letter and IOU document again for a second, then shakes his head*) No, nightmare ... (*He rips both letters and the IOU document, throws them into the stove and watches them burn*)

Silence

Since Christmas Eve? Three days?
Nora Yes. Three long days.
Torvald And you thought the only way out ...? It doesn't matter. It's over. Nora, it's over, done with. Nora, let it sink in. Say it.

She stares at him, frozen

I've forgiven you. You don't realize that, do you? Oh, believe me, giddy girl, I've forgiven you. I understand why. Love. For me.
Nora Yes. That's true.
Torvald A wife's love. Real love. You went about it the wrong way, you're an innocent, you didn't know, how could you? No, come to me. So you need me to steer your course? — that's the way of things. You're a woman, defenceless? — I don't love you less because of that, I love you more. Forget what I said. I panicked. I thought I'd been demolished. I've forgiven you, Nora. I swear to God, I've forgiven you.
Nora Thank you for your forgiveness.

She moves towards her room

Torvald Where are you going?

Nora To get out of fancy-dress.

She exits to her room

Torvald Yes. Then you can rest. You had a scare, catch your breath now. I'll keep you warm. (*He hovers about Nora's doorway*) Our home: your sanctuary. Lie low here, turtle-dove. The hawk's dead, the hunt is over, I've freed you. You'll see that, tomorrow. You'll wake up safe in the nest and know you're forgiven. And we'll go back to where we were. As if I couldn't forgive you? As if I could shut you out? Nora: you're blameless. Deep down, I've forgiven you. You don't know what that feels like for me, as a man; I tell you, it's the most gratifying feeling in the world, because you're mine twice over now: you're my wife, and my child. Yes. It feels like I've brought you into the world. My own innocent. Don't be scared, you're safe, I'll protect you; all you have to do is tell me what you want when you want it, and my head will think for yours, my heart will beat for yours ...

Nora appears, in day dress

Dressed?
Nora Yes.
Torvald But it's so late?
Nora I'm not going to bed tonight.
Torvald Nora?
Nora It's not that late. Sit down, Torvald, I have to talk to you.
Torvald Why so cold ...? Your eyes, they're ——
Nora Sit.
Torvald I don't understand?
Nora No. That's right. You don't. And I've never understood you. Not till now. Don't interrupt. Just listen. Time for plain-speaking, Torvald.
Torvald I don't follow.

Silence

Nora What a thing. The two of us. Sitting here.
Torvald What of it?
Nora Eight years. Husband and wife. And this is the first time we've had a serious conversation.
Torvald "Serious?" What do you mean?
Nora Eight years, and we've never seriously discussed serious things.
Torvald Like what, my day-to-day concerns? You couldn't do much about most of those.
Nora Not "your concerns". No. We've never sat down and tried to get to the bottom of anything.

Torvald But that isn't quite you, is it, Nora?

Nora You see, Torvald, you don't know me at all. You've done me a severe injustice. First Pa, then you.

Torvald What? We've loved you more than anyone else in the world.

Nora You've never loved me. The idea of loving me has been lots of fun.

Torvald You're not serious?

Nora Yes, I am. Back at home, Pa used to tell me all about the things he believed in, and because he believed in them, I believed in them, so if I did feel differently about something I'd keep it secret because I knew he'd get angry. Pa played with me, like I was his toy; just like I played with *my* toys. And then I came here to your house ——

Torvald You see our marriage like —?

Nora —— when Pa turned me over to you — and here, this furniture, everything — was *you*, not me; but because it was you, it became me; or I played make-believe, I'm not sure — perhaps I played make-believe so much it *did* become me. I look back now, and I realize I've been living like a beggar. Getting by by acting out tricks. Because that's what you asked for. You and Pa have committed a terrible sin against me. I've made nothing of myself. And that's your fault.

Torvald I've never heard anything so selfish. You've been happy here?

Nora No.

Torvald What?

Nora I thought so, but no. I've laughed, but I haven't been happy. You've been very kind. But make-believe is make-believe, isn't it? This place is a nursery, Torvald. I was Pa's play-daughter, and I'm your play-wife. And Ivor and Emmy, they're my play-children, and everybody thinks it's so much fun.

Torvald You're exaggerating, emotional ——

Nora No. It's the truth.

Torvald If — if — there's something in it, well now things will change. Play-time's over. Time to grow up, to learn.

Nora Learn? Me, or the children?

Torvald Both.

Nora Torvald. You're not the man to teach me to be a grown-up; you can't teach me to be the right wife for you.

Torvald How can you say that?

Nora And I don't have what it takes to teach my little ones anything.

Torvald is speechless

You said it yourself. You don't trust me with them.

Torvald I was furious, forget that!

Nora But you meant it. And it's true, I'm not up to it. Not yet, not till I've seen to something else. I need to grow up, on my own; to learn, *myself.* You can't help, it's down to *me.* And so that's why I'm leaving you tonight.

Torvald is on his feet at once

Torvald What?

Nora It's time for me to stand on my own feet. Time to get to grips with myself. To get to the bottom of things. Out there. So I can't live with you a second longer.

Torvald Nora ...!

Nora I'll go straight away. Kristine'll give me a bed for the night.

Torvald You're mad — no, never, no, I forbid it.

Nora Oh, Torvald, there's no point to that now. I'm going to take my things, and go, and never ask for anything from you again. I'll go home. Home-home, my old town. I'll find something to do there.

Torvald You're ill, this is insane. You can't see what you're doing. You don't know anything.

Nora But I want to know something.

Torvald You belong here. With your husband, your children. Think, Nora what will people say?

Nora I don't care about that. I only know I've got to do this. I've got no choice.

Torvald Exactly, no choice: your duty is *here.*

Nora My "duty". What is that?

Torvald What do you think?

Nora I don't know.

Torvald For God's sake, your obligations towards me and our son and our daughter. Sacred.

Nora I have other duties.

Torvald *Sacred.*

Nora Duties to myself.

Torvald You're a mother and a wife above everything else.

Nora I don't believe that now. Above everything else I'm a human being. Just like you. I've got to try to be one, anyway. I know a lot of people see it like you, and books say it, but that's not good enough for me now. I've got to sort through all of this for myself.

Torvald God then. Look to Him. Your religion.

Nora I don't even know what religion is, Torvald.

Torvald What?

Nora I only know what Pastor Hansen said in confirmation classes. Religion's such-and-such and so-and-so. Once I'm out of here and by myself, I'll look into all that as well. I want to see if Pastor Hansen had it right. Actually, no, is it right for me?

Torvald I can't take all this in. You're so young. Forget God, what about your conscience? Morality. Hmn? Or are you empty inside?

Nora I should have an answer, I suppose. But I don't. It's a muddle. All I know is you talk about all that in your way, and I hear a language I don't know how to speak. We're not the same. And the law: I had that all wrong. A woman doesn't have the right to spare her dying father—no she doesn't. She's not allowed to save her husband. I don't think those things can be true.

Torvald You're a baby. A fool. This is how we live. Society.

Nora What is that? And who's right? Me, or society? I've got to find out.

Torvald You're sick in the head. You've lost all reason.

Nora I've never felt so clear and certain as I do tonight.

Torvald Certain you can leave your husband and son and daughter?

Nora Yes.

Torvald Then there's only one explanation.

Nora Yes?

Torvald You don't love me anymore.

Nora Yes. I don't love you.

Torvald Nora ... Nora ...

Nora Oh, Torvald, I'm sad, because you've been very kind. But I don't love you anymore.

Torvald How? When?

Nora Tonight. It didn't happen. The miraculous something didn't happen. And I realized you're not the man I thought you were.

Torvald What are you talking about? — I don't ...

Nora I've waited and waited for this miraculous—wondrous—something. Seven years. Good God, I knew it wasn't going to happen any old day of the week. Then I got myself into this tangle, and it strangled me, so tight, and I thought for sure, now, now it will happen— miraculously happen— it *has to*. Krogstad's letter was in the box — and not for one second did I think you'd crumble before that man. I was sure — positive — you wouldn't let him beat you, positive you'd say, "Tell the world, tell the whole wide world". And after that ——

Torvald After my wife had been dishonoured and disgraced?

Nora — after that, I was positive you'd stand up and say, "It's me, I'm to blame, I'm guilty".

Torvald Nora ——

Nora Yes I know, of course I wouldn't have let you do that for me (though what's my word against yours?). Anyway, that was the miraculous something. I prayed for it, it was terrifying, and I'd have killed myself to stop it.

Torvald I'd work my whole life for you. I'd put up with heartbreak, misery. But no man gives up his *honour*, even for the person he loves.

Nora A hundred thousand women have.

Torvald You talk and think like an ignorant child.

Nora So I do? The way *you* talk and think is — I could never *ever* spend my life with ... When the panic was over, *your* panic, when your heart had come out of your mouth — you made it seem as if nothing had happened. Little Nora was your lark again, your play-thing, twice as tender, twice as feeble. That was it. I realized then. I don't know you at all. Seven years with a stranger. Two children with a stranger. God, it makes my blood run cold, I could rip myself to bits ——

Torvald Nora ... Please ... I see. I see it now. Stop—reach out to me, please.

Nora I can't be your wife like this, I'm not your wife.

Torvald I can change.

Nora Maybe, once you don't have your play-thing.

Torvald I don't want to lose you. I can't imagine life without you.

Nora All the more reason.

She goes to her room and returns with a coat and small bag. She puts on her coat, hat and shawl

Torvald Wait till tomorrow ——

Nora I can't spend the night in a strange man's house.

Torvald — as brother and sister ... We don't have to ...

Nora Don't delude yourself. Goodbye, Torvald. I don't want to see my boy or my little girl. They're in better hands than mine. I'm no good to them as I am today.

Torvald Nora, one day ... One day?

Nora I don't know, do I? I've got no idea what's going to happen to me.

Torvald You're my wife — always ...

Nora Enough, Torvald. I do know something about the law. When a wife leaves her husband's house, he has no responsibilities towards her. I know this. He's set free. I'm leaving, Torvald, so you're free. As I am. There's nothing to bind us. We're both free.

She takes off her ring and presses it into his hand

Give me mine.

He shakes his head

Do it.

He gives her his ring

Yes. (*She puts her keys down*) Anne-Marie knows how to run the house, she knows more than I do. After I've gone home, Kristine will come round to pack my things, the things I owned before we were married. I'll have them sent on.

Torvald Will you ever think of me?

Nora Yes, I think I will. Often. And the children. And this house.

Torvald Can I write?

Nora No.

Torvald Let me send ...?

Nora Nothing.

Torvald But if you ever needed something, I could help ...

Nora I won't say it again. I don't accept help from strangers.

Torvald Will I ever be more ...?

Nora Oh, Torvald, for that we'd need something rare. Something miraculous.

Torvald What, *what is that?*

Nora Both of us — we'd both have to change so much that — I don't believe in anything miraculous now, Torvald.

Torvald I can, I can believe ... Change so much that ——?

Nora That we could share a life that was a real marriage. Goodbye.

She exits through the hall

Torvald Nora. Nora.

Silence

(*Hopefully*) Something rare? Something miraculous?

The street door slams

FURNITURE AND PROPERTY LIST

ACT I

On stage: Tasteful but modest furnishings including chairs and a table
Stove
Piano
In hallway: Christmas tree; basket containing Christmas decorations
including sweets, fruit, money, candles and red ribbons
On front door: glass-fronted letter-box
Embroidery, needle and thread
*In **Torvald**'s study door*: key

Off stage: Parcels (**Nora**)
Children's paintings (**Ivor and Emmy**)
Bundle of papers (**Torvald**)

Personal: **Nora**: bag of macaroons; watch; wedding-ring
Torvald: pen; wallet containing money; wedding-ring
Krogstad: piece of paper

ACT II

Set: Christmas Tree stripped of decorations
Nora's overcoat on chair

Off stage: Large cardboard box containing costumes; 1 glove; Italian tarantella
dress; silk flesh-coloured stockings; tambourine; coloured shawl
(**Anne-Marie**)
Lamp (**Anne-Marie**)
Visiting card (**Anne-Marie**)
Bundle of papers including an envelope (**Torvald**)
Personal: **Krogstad**: letter

ACT III

Strike: Cardboard box and costumes

Set: Several envelopes (1 containing letter), two visiting cards and hairpin
in letter-box
Box of cigars with matches and cigar trimmer

Off stage: Small bag (**Nora**)
                Envelope containing letter and document (**Anne-Marie**)

Personal: **Torvald**: house keys
                Nora: house keys

LIGHTING PLOT

Practical fittings required: nil
1 interior setting with adjoining hall leading to front door. Same throughout

ACT I. Christmas Eve. Morning

To open: general interior lighting

No cues

ACT II. Christmas Day. Early evening

To open: general interior lighting

Cue 1	**Nora** stands at the doorway to the hall	(Page 30)
	Start slow fade	

Cue 2	**Anne-Marie** enters with a lamp	(Page 33)
	Covering spot on lamp. Brighten interior lighting	

ACT III. Boxing Day. Evening

To open: low interior lighting. Covering spot on lamp

Cue 3	**Torvald** exits to his study	(Page 45)
	Flickering candle light from the study	

EFFECTS PLOT

ACT I

Cue 1   **Nora:** " ... I want to ——"   (Page 4)
           Doorbell ring

ACT II

Cue 2   **Nora:** " ... Get out of it. Somehow."   (Page 30)
           Doorbell ring

ACT III

Cue 3   To open ACT III   (Page 42)
           Dance music from the floor above

Cue 4   **Torvald:** " Nothing except — this."   (Page 51)
           Doorbell ring

Lightning Source UK Ltd.
Milton Keynes UK
UKOW06f0342180817
307512UK00001B/32/P

9 780573 019517